First World War
and Army of Occupation
War Diary
France, Belgium and Germany

14 DIVISION
41 Infantry Brigade,
Brigade Machine Gun Company
28 January 1916 - 28 February 1918

WO95/1896/4

The Naval & Military Press Ltd
www.nmarchive.com
Published in association with The National Archives

Published by

The Naval & Military Press Ltd

Unit 10 Ridgewood Industrial Park,
Uckfield, East Sussex,
TN22 5QE England
Tel: +44 (0) 1825 749494

www.naval-military-press.com
www.nmarchive.com

This diary has been reprinted in facsimile from the original. Any imperfections are inevitably reproduced and the quality may fall short of modern type and cartographic standards.

© **Crown Copyright**
Images reproduced by permission of The National Archives, London, England, 2015.

Contents

Document type	Place/Title	Date From	Date To
Heading	1896/4		
Heading	14th Division 41st Infy Bde 41st Machine Gun Coy Feb 1916-Feb 1918		
Heading	War Diary Of 41st Infantry Brigade Machine Gun Co. From 15th February 1916 To 30th April, 1916 Volume I Feb 18		
War Diary	Winnezeele	15/02/1916	29/02/1916
War Diary	Arras	01/03/1916	30/04/1916
Miscellaneous	D.A.G. G.H.Q. 3rd Echelon Base	31/05/1916	31/05/1916
War Diary	Arras	03/05/1916	04/05/1916
War Diary	Agnes Les Duisans	09/05/1916	09/05/1916
War Diary	Duisans	10/05/1916	10/05/1916
War Diary	Aubigny	14/05/1916	22/05/1916
War Diary	Mont St Eloy	23/05/1916	27/05/1916
Miscellaneous	D.A.G. 3rd Echelon Base	01/08/1916	01/08/1916
War Diary	Arras	01/07/1916	28/07/1916
War Diary	Agnez-Les-Duisans	29/07/1916	31/07/1916
Heading	41st Brigade 14th Division 41st Brigade Machine Gun Company August 1916		
Heading	War Diary Of 41st Brigade Machine Gun Coy. From 1st August, 1916 To 31st August, 1916 Volume VI.		
War Diary	Occoches	01/08/1916	01/08/1916
War Diary	Bretel	02/08/1916	08/08/1916
War Diary	Dernancourt	08/08/1916	30/08/1916
War Diary	Croquoison	31/08/1916	31/08/1916
Heading	War Diary Of 41st Brigade Machine Gun Co. From: 1st September, 1916 To: 30th September, 1916 Volume VII		
War Diary	Croquoison	01/09/1916	10/09/1916
War Diary	Dernancourt	13/09/1916	13/09/1916
War Diary	Montauban	14/09/1916	17/09/1916
War Diary	Dernancourt	20/09/1916	21/09/1916
War Diary	Grouches	23/09/1916	25/09/1916
War Diary	Beaumetz	26/09/1916	26/09/1916
War Diary	Le Fermont	27/09/1916	30/09/1916
Heading	War Diary Of 41st Brigade Machine Gun Coy. From: 1st October, 1916 To: 31st October, 1916 Volume VIII		
War Diary	Le Fermont	01/10/1916	24/10/1916
War Diary	Berneville	24/10/1916	30/10/1916
Heading	War Diary Of 41st Brigade Machine Gun Compy. From: 1st November, 1916 To 30th November, 1916 Volume IX.		
War Diary	Grand Roullecourt	04/11/1916	24/11/1916
Heading	War Diary Of 41st Brigade Machine Gun Company. From 1st December, 1916 To 31st December, 1916 Volume XV		
War Diary	Liencourt	01/12/1916	14/12/1916
War Diary	Monchiet	15/12/1916	15/12/1916
War Diary	Le Fermont	19/12/1916	31/12/1916
War Diary	The Line	28/01/1916	29/01/1916

Heading	War Diary Of 41st Brigade Machine Gun Company. From: 1st January, 1917 To 31st January, 1917 Volume XI		
War Diary	Le Fermont	01/01/1917	31/01/1917
Heading	War Diary Of 41st Brigade Machine Gun Company From: 1st February, 1917 To 28th February 1917 Volume XII		
War Diary	Le Fermont	01/02/1917	01/02/1917
War Diary	Beaumetz	03/02/1917	03/02/1917
War Diary	Sambrin	05/02/1917	10/02/1917
War Diary	Berneville	11/02/1917	19/02/1917
War Diary	Berneville	23/02/1917	28/02/1917
Heading	War Diary Of 41st Machine Gun Company From 1st March 1917 To 31st March 1917 Volume XIII		
War Diary	Berneville	01/03/1917	01/03/1917
War Diary	Sombrin	02/03/1917	22/03/1917
War Diary	Berneville	23/03/1917	24/03/1917
War Diary	Arras	28/03/1917	30/03/1917
Heading	War Diary Of 41st Machine Gun Coy. From April 1st 1917 To April 30th 1917 Volume 14		
War Diary	Arras	01/04/1917	04/04/1917
War Diary	Ronville	05/04/1917	10/04/1917
War Diary	Cojeul Switch	10/04/1917	13/04/1917
War Diary	Arras	14/04/1917	15/04/1917
War Diary	Sombrin	16/04/1917	28/04/1917
Map	Map A To Accompany 14th Division Operation Order No.112		
Map			
Map	Map B To Accompany 14th Division Operation Order No. 113		
Heading	41st MG Coy War Diary For May 1917 From 1st May 1917 To 31st May 1917 Volume XV		
War Diary	Wancourt	01/05/1917	24/05/1917
War Diary	Beauraines	25/05/1917	31/05/1917
Heading	War Diary 41st M.G. Coy June 1917		
War Diary	Beaurains	01/06/1917	02/06/1917
War Diary	Wancourt	04/06/1917	07/06/1917
War Diary	Beaurains	09/06/1917	10/06/1917
War Diary	Beaumetz	11/06/1917	11/06/1917
War Diary	Gaudiempre	12/06/1917	12/06/1917
War Diary	Louvencourt	13/06/1917	30/06/1917
Heading	War Diary July 1917 41st M.G. Coy Volume XVII		
War Diary	Louvencourt	01/07/1917	01/07/1917
War Diary	Beauval	10/07/1917	10/07/1917
War Diary	Doullens	11/07/1917	11/07/1917
War Diary	Berthen	12/07/1917	31/07/1917
Heading	War Diary 41st M.G. Coy. August 1917 Volume XVIII		
War Diary	Berthen	01/08/1917	06/08/1917
War Diary	Hondeghem	15/08/1917	15/08/1917
War Diary	Dickebusch	16/08/1917	16/08/1917
War Diary	Hooge	18/08/1917	19/08/1917
War Diary	Chateau Segard	20/08/1917	21/08/1917
War Diary	Hooge	22/08/1917	23/08/1917
War Diary	Dickebusch	24/08/1917	30/08/1917
Heading	War Diary September 1917 41st M.G. Coy Volume XIX		

War Diary	Meteren	01/09/1917	02/09/1917
War Diary	Neuve Eglise	04/09/1917	10/09/1917
War Diary	Messines	11/09/1917	20/09/1917
War Diary	Neuve Eglise	23/09/1917	29/09/1917
Heading	41st M.G. Coy War Diary October 1917 Volume XX		
War Diary	Neuve Eglise	01/10/1917	01/10/1917
War Diary	Reninghelst	06/10/1917	08/10/1917
War Diary	Micmac Camp	09/10/1917	10/10/1917
War Diary	Ridgewood	11/10/1917	12/10/1917
War Diary	Gheluvelt	13/10/1917	17/10/1917
War Diary	Ridge Wood	18/10/1917	20/10/1917
War Diary	Chippawa	21/10/1917	21/10/1917
War Diary	Meteren	23/10/1917	31/10/1917
Heading	War Diary 41st M.G. Coy Nov 30/17 Volume XXI		
War Diary	Meterin	01/10/1917	11/11/1917
War Diary	Val D'Acquin	12/11/1917	30/11/1917
Heading	41st M.G. Coy War Diary December 1917 Volume XXII		
War Diary	Goldfish Chateau	01/12/1917	02/12/1917
War Diary	Wieltje	03/12/1917	03/12/1917
War Diary	Wieltje And The Line	04/12/1917	09/12/1917
War Diary	Brandhoek	10/12/1917	14/12/1917
War Diary	Wieltje And The Line	14/12/1917	21/12/1917
War Diary	Junction Camp	21/12/1917	25/12/1917
War Diary	Val D'Acquin	26/12/1917	31/12/1917
Heading	41st Machine Gun Coy War Diary January 1918 Volume XXIII		
War Diary	Val D'Acquin	01/01/1918	02/01/1918
War Diary	Tatinghem	03/01/1918	03/01/1918
War Diary	Sailly-Le-Sec	04/01/1918	22/01/1918
War Diary	Fresnoy-En-Chaussee	23/01/1918	23/01/1918
War Diary	Roye	24/01/1918	24/01/1918
War Diary	Beines	25/01/1918	25/01/1918
War Diary	Jussy	26/01/1918	27/01/1918
Heading	War Diary February 1918 41st M.G. Coy Volume XXIV		
War Diary	Line	01/02/1918	24/02/1918
War Diary	In The Line	24/02/1918	28/02/1918

4/9/14

14TH DIVISION
41ST INFY BDE

41ST MACHINE GUN COY.
FEB 1916 – FEB 1918

CONFIDENTIAL.

WAR DIARY
- of -
41st INFANTRY BRIGADE MACHINE GUN Co.

From: 15th February, 1916.
To: 30th April, 1916.

Volume I.

Army Form C. 2118.

WAR DIARY
or
INTELLIGENCE SUMMARY.
(Erase heading not required.)

Place	Date	Hour	Summary of Events and Information	Remarks and references to Appendices
CASSEZELE	15/2/16		A 1st Bde. Machine Gun Company formed. Major A.P. Evans 7th Bn. KRRC. appointed to Command the Company. Lieut. L.P.B. Thomson from 7th Bn Rifle Brigade appointed Second in Command	
CASSEZELE	17/2/16		The Commander in Chief inspected the Company	1 App.
CASSEZELE	18/2/16		G.O.C. /4 Division inspected the Company.	1 App.
	24/2/16		Entrained at CASSEL & proceeded to LONGEAU near AMIENS. From here the Company proceeded by Motor buses to FLESSELLES (13 miles).	1 App.
	29/2/16		Marched to DOULLENS (12 miles)	1 App.
	25/2/16		Marched to WARLUZEL (10 miles). Great difficulty was experienced in getting the transport along owing to the snow	1 App.
	29/2/16		Marched to ARRAS (15 miles)	1 App.

Evans Major
O.C. 1st Bde M.G. Coy

Army Form C. 2118.

WAR DIARY
or
INTELLIGENCE SUMMARY.
(Erase heading not required.)

Instructions regarding War Diaries and Intelligence Summaries are contained in F. S. Regs., Part II. and the Staff Manual respectively. Title pages will be prepared in manuscript.

Place	Date	Hour	Summary of Events and Information	Remarks and references to Appendices
ARRAS	March 1916 1st		General reconnaissance of the trenches by the Officers under the guidance of the French Mitrailleuse Officers	Appx
"	2nd		Relieved the Mitrailleuse Companies of the 11th and 20th Regiments d'Infanterie. The Company took over 16 out of the 24 emplacements which the French occupied	Appx
"	5th		Divisional front re-organised 4 guns on the right were relieved by the 42nd Bde M.G. Coy & went to rest	Appx
"	6th		Lieut L.E. Netcott & 2/Lieut Pigott arrived from M.G. Corps to make up establishment	Appx
"	7-31st		at ARRAS in the trenches	Appx
ARRAS	April 1-5		at ARRAS in the trenches	Appx
"	6		2/Lieut Rodway & 2/Lt Roddick wounded	Appx
"	6-30		at ARRAS in the trenches	Appx

Haws Lieut. & R.S. Coy
O.C. H¹

D.A.G. G.H.Q. 3rd Echelon Rouen

XIV

Herewith War Diary of 41st Bde. M.G. Coy
for month of May

VOL 3

L P B Sherman
Lt
for O.C. 41st Bde. M.G. Coy

31/5/16.

41 BM 7th 5 Army Form C. 2118.

WAR DIARY
or
INTELLIGENCE SUMMARY.
(Erase heading not required.)

Place	Date	Hour	Summary of Events and Information	Remarks and references to Appendices
ARRAS	May 1916 3rd		The 95th Inf. Bde. M.G. Coy arrived at ARRAS	LPBM
	4th		The Officers of the 95th Inf. Bde M.G. Coy reconnoitred the line. The Company was relieved by the 95th Bde M.G.Coy. The Company marched to AGNES LES DUISANS (5 miles)	LPBM
AGNES LES DUISANS	9th		2nd Lt E L BARTLEMAN joined the company from GRANTHAM	LPBM
	10th		The Company marched to AUBIGNY (5 miles)	LPBM
AUBIGNY	14th		The Officers reconnoitred the Gefe Line & the Army line	LPBM
	15th		The Company began work on the Army line	LPBM
	19th		2nd Lt F W PORTEOUS joined the company from GRANTHAM	LPBM
	20th		2nd Lt C B WOOD joined the company having been posted from 8th Bn. Rifle Brigade	LPBM
	22nd	1.30 am	The company marched to MONT ST ELOY (6 miles) where they remained in readiness 6 hrs up to the line.	LPBM
MONT ST ELOY	23rd		2nd Lt A R RODNAY rejoined the Company from ETAPLES.	LPBM
	26th		The Brigadier inspected the Company.	LPBM
	27th		The Company marched to ACQ (2 miles)	LPBM

D.A.G.
   3rd Echelon
      Base

Herewith War Diary of the 41st Inf. Brigade Machine Gun Company for the month of July.

1/8/16

LPB Merriam
   Lt
for O.C. 41st Bde. M.G. Coy

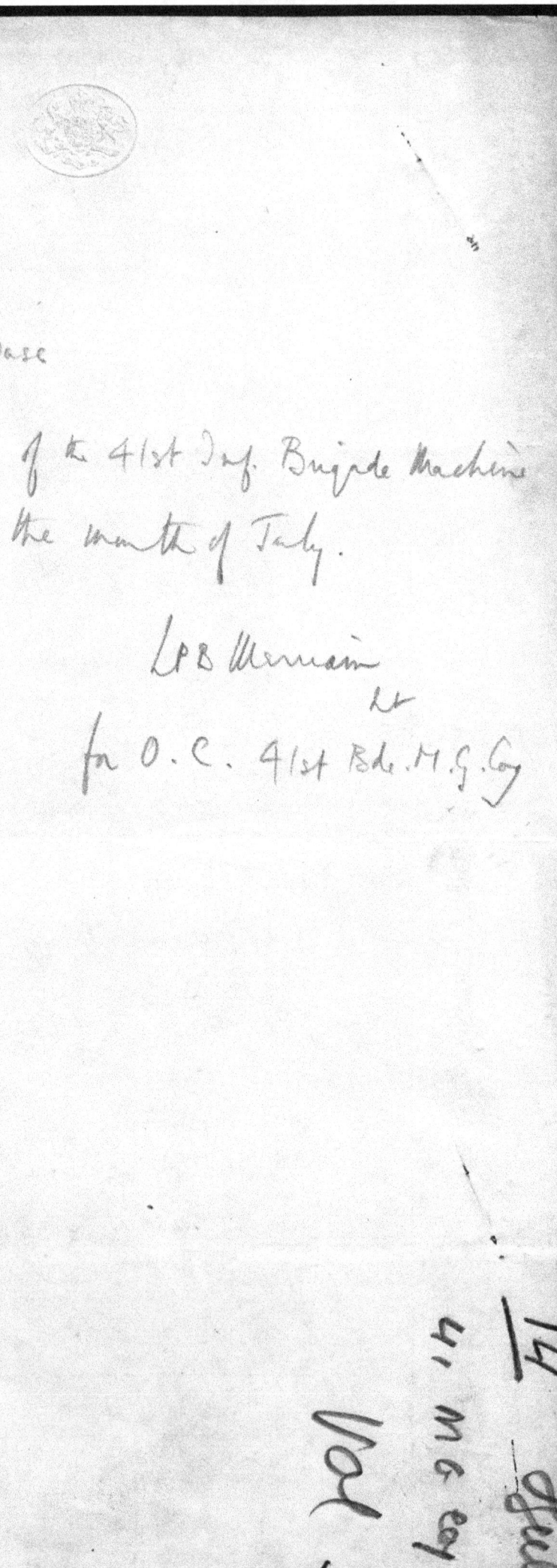

Army Form C. 2118.

WAR DIARY
or
INTELLIGENCE SUMMARY.
(Erase heading not required.)

Instructions regarding War Diaries and Intelligence Summaries are contained in F. S. Regs, Part II. and the Staff Manual respectively. Title pages will be prepared in manuscript.

Place	Date	Hour	Summary of Events and Information	Remarks and references to Appendices
ARRAS	July 1918 1st		The Germans flew up a mine in K.2. Sector. Two guns were sent up to the place of the crater to protect it from attack	APP.
	27th 28th		On trenches with the K Sector at ARRAS	APP.
	28th		Three guns of TA 110th Brigade Machine Gun Company relieved two guns of the 64th Brigade Machine Gun Company which relieved the Company. The Company	APP.
AGNEZ-LES-DUISANS	29th		marched to AGNEZ-LES-DUISANS (5 miles)	APP.
	30th		The Company marched to GRAND RULLECOURT (9 miles). The halt was very great	APP.
	31st		The Company marched to OCCOCHES (12 miles). Again the heat was very great	APP.

41st Brigade.
14th Division.

41st BRIGADE

MACHINE GUN COMPANY

AUGUST 1916

CONFIDENTIAL.

WAR DIARY

- of -

41st BRIGADE MACHINE GUN Coy.

From: 1st August, 1916 - To: 31st August, 1916.

Volume VI.

WAR DIARY
or
INTELLIGENCE SUMMARY.
(Erase heading not required.)

Army Form C. 2118.

Vol. No 6

Place	Date	Hour	Summary of Events and Information	Remarks and references to Appendices
OCCOCHES	August 1916 1st		The Company marched to BRETEL (4 miles)	Appx.
BRETEL	2nd to 6th		The Company practised the attack and Wood fighting.	Appx.
	7th		The Company marched to CANDAS (5 miles).	Appx.
	8th	1 A.M.	The Company entrained at CANDAS & proceeded to MERICOURT, where they detrained at 7 A.M. From there the Company marched to DERNANCOURT (7 miles). 2 Officers reconnoitred the line held by the 50th Brigade Machine gun Company, between DELVILLE WOOD & HIGH WOOD.	Appx.
DERNANCOURT	11th		The Company relieved the 50th Bde Machine Gun Company. 1 O.R. wounded. 2/Lt J. N. Head joined the Company	Appx.
	12th			Appx.
	18th		The Company took part in the attack on ORCHARD TRENCH & WOOD LANE. The 7th Bn. Kings Royal Rifles & the 7th Bn. Rifle Brigade assaulted at 2.45 P.M. & took ORCHARD TRENCH & part of WOOD LANE. About 9 P.M. from machine guns under 2/Lt A.C. MEREDITH & 2/Lt F.N. PORTEOUS went up to the Captured Trench & consolidated. Six machine guns kept up barrage (indirect fire) on the enemy communication trenches & tracks as far as the SWITCH TRENCH & in some cases beyond it. The fire of the guns	

WAR DIARY
or
INTELLIGENCE SUMMARY
(Erase heading not required.)

Army Form C. 2118.

No 6 (Continued)

Place	Date	Hour	Summary of Events and Information	Remarks and references to Appendices
	August 1916			
	18th Continued		was maintained both before the attack & for six hours afterwards. Two O.R. were killed & 4 O.R. wounded.	LPPA
	19th		The 100th Brigade Machine Gun Company relieved the Company. About 8.30 PM, just before the Company was relieved, the enemy put up an intense artillery barrage & was reported to be massing for an attack. Six machine guns immediately put up a barrage on & the same targets as the previous day.	LPPA
			4 Vickers guns relieved those of the 43rd Bde. Machine Gun Company on our right in DEVILS TRENCH & DELVILLE WOOD.	LPPA
	21st		The Company relieved the 42nd Bde. Machine Gun Company to the right of DELVILLE WOOD.	LPPA
			The 42nd Bn. M.G.Cy took over the four guns in DELVILLE WOOD in DEVILS TRENCH.	LPPA
			The 61st Infantry Brigade were on our right.	
	22nd		2/Lt H.A. WALKER was evacuated, sick to Hospital. 2/Lt C.B. WOOD returned to England having been dismissed from His Majesty's service by sentence of F.G.C.M.	LPPA
	23rd		2/Lt A.H. GILBERT joined the Company. One O.R. killed, no O.R. wounded	LPPA
	24th		The Company assisted in the attack of the 42nd Infantry Brigade on the edge of DELVILLE WOOD & in the demonstration of the 41st & 2nd Bdes. by indirect fire from four machine

WAR DIARY
or
INTELLIGENCE SUMMARY.
(Erase heading not required.)

Army Form C. 2118.

No 6 (continued)

Place	Date	Hour	Summary of Events and Information	Remarks and references to Appendices
	August 1916 24th continued		Gun on the Enemy Communication trenches and tracks. Three O.R. wounded.	Appx
	25th		Four O.R. wounded & one gun destroyed by shell fire	Appx
	26th		The 22nd Brigade Machine Gun Company relieved the Company. One gun was destroyed and two O.R. wounded. The Company on relief marched to DERNANCOURT (10 miles)	Appx
DERNANCOURT	28th		2/Lt J.H.T.C. DEVEY, 2/Lt A.C.M. DYMOCK & 2/Lt J.N. DENNIS joined the Company & Lt L.E. NOTCUTT left the Company on appointment to the 27th Bde. M.G. Coy as Second in Command.	Appx
	29th			Appx
	30th		The Company (less the transport) marched to ALBERT (4 miles). They entrained there & proceeded to KARRAINES via AMIENS and LONGRE. They detrained at ARRAINES & marched to CROQUOISON 4 miles. The Transport proceeded by road as far as St SAUVEUR.	Appx
CROQUOISON	31st		The Transport reached CROQUOISON about 5 p.m.	Appx

J.R. Warriner Lt
A/Lt Pde M.G. Coy.

CONFIDENTIAL.

WAR DIARY

-of-

41st BRIGADE MACHINE GUN Co.

From: 1st September, 1916.
To: 30th September, 1916.

Volume VII.

WAR DIARY
or
INTELLIGENCE SUMMARY.

Army Form C. 2118.

141st Bty 5 & 6
Vol VII

Place	Date	Hour	Summary of Events and Information	Remarks and references to Appendices
Longueau	1/9/16		Company rested at Longueau	Sny S
"	8/9/16		Transport left Longueau for DERNANCOURT.	Sny S
"	10/9/16		Company entrained for DERNANCOURT via AMIENS. Company took over from 166th and 164th Companies between	Sny S
DERNANCOURT	13/9/16		DELVILLE WOOD and GINCHY	Sny S
MAUBAN	14/9/16		One gun KILLED, 3 O.R. wounded. The Company took part in the attack on FLERS.	
MAUBAN	15/9/16		1 Officer 2/Lt GILBERT A.H. wounded, 1 O.R. killed, 2 O.R. wounded	
"			1 O.R. missing. 2 guns put out of action.	Sny S
"	16/9/16		Attack continued. Lieut L.P.B. MERRIAM wounded 4 O.R. wounded	Sny S
"	17/9/16		The Company relieved by (21st Division) and then proceeded to FRICOURT CAMP rested for 10 hours	
"			and then marched to billets at DERNANCOURT.	Sny S
DERNANCOURT	20/9/16		Transport moved off by road to GROUCHES arrived 21/9/16	and
"	21/9/16		The Company entrained in the morn ALBERT - AMIENS. Road and proceeded to GROUCHES arriving at 5 P.M.	Sny S

WAR DIARY or INTELLIGENCE SUMMARY

Army Form C. 2118.

41st B. M. G. Coy.

Place	Date	Hour	Summary of Events and Information	Remarks and references to Appendices
	July			
OUCHEL	28/7/16		2/Lt M.K. MAGGS joined the company from Machine Gun Corps base	S.A.E.
	27/7/16		The company & transport moved to BEAUMETZ, an LS 97 E.v.X. 14 miles	Jus
BAUMETZ	28/7/16		The company marched to LE FERMONT and relieved the 37th Brigade Machine Gun Coy in the ARRAS & Lator	One
			One O.R. wounded accidentally (rifle wound)	
FERMONT	29/7/16		One O.R. killed (shell dam)	O.R.S
	30th	2.R	Lieut N.F.M LITTLE Machine Gun Corps arrived to take over second in command of the company	Sy.S

CONFIDENTIAL.

WAR DIARY

- of -

41st BRIGADE MACHINE GUN Coy.

From: 1st October, 1916.
To: 31st October, 1916.

Volume VIII.

WAR DIARY

Army Form C. 2118.

41st. B. M.G. Coy.

Place	Date	Hour	Summary of Events and Information	Remarks and references to Appendices
FERMONT	1-10-16		Company in trenches.	W.J.M.Z.
"	3/10/16		Relief of section from front line to reserve and vice versa.	W.J.M.Z.
"	4/10/16		Enemy machine gun fire was retaliated upon by two of our guns during the night. 4000 rounds were fired, and enemy fire entirely ceased.	W.J.M.Z.
	5/10/16		4000 rounds again fired during night.	W.J.M.Z.
	6/10/16		M.G. commenced on a concrete emplacement near PETIT CHATEAU.	W.J.M.Z.
	8/10/16		Heavy rifle and machine-gun fire from enemy between 9.30 and 10 p.m. owing to a working party being mistaken for a raid. One O.R. wounded.	W.J.M.Z.
	10/10/16		Inter-section relief as on 3rd Oct.	W.J.M.Z.
	15/10/16		Lieut. E.M. Gurney left the company on appointment as 2nd in Command to 68th M.G. Company.	W.J.M.Z.
	16/10/16		Inter-section relief.	W.J.M.Z.
	20/10/16		Some heavy shells fired into WAILLY, bringing down a wall in FRENCH ST.	W.J.M.Z.
	24/10/16		41st M.G. Coy. Relief - Coy-M.G. on FRENCH ST. Company relieved by 37th Coy. Relief was completed by 9.0.	W.J.M.Z.

W.J.G. for Lieut.
O.C. 41st. M.G. Coy.

Army Form C. 2118.

WAR DIARY
or
INTELLIGENCE SUMMARY.
(Erase heading not required.)

Place	Date	Hour	Summary of Events and Information	Remarks and references to Appendices
BERNEVILLE	24/10/16		incident by 11.15 p.m. On whit company withdrew to BERNEVILLE	2)/M.2
	25/10/16		Major A. P. Evans relinquished command of company.	2/-/M.2
	26/10/16		Company marched from BERNEVILLE via BARLY and SOMBRIN to GRAND RULLECOURT.	2/M.2
	27/10/16		Company in training at GRAND RULLECOURT.	2/-/M.2
	30/10/16		Lieut. D. E. Isaac joined and assumed command of company.	2/-/M.2

H.J.M.Libb Lieut.
for O.C. 41st M.J. Cy.

CONFIDENTIAL.

WAR DIARY

- of -

41st BRIGADE MACHINE GUN Compy.

From: 1st November, 1916.
To: 30th November, 1916.

Volume IX.

Army Form C. 2118.

WAR DIARY
or
INTELLIGENCE SUMMARY

41st M.G. Coy

(Erase heading not required.)

Place	Date	Hour	Summary of Events and Information	Remarks and references to Appendices
RAND OULLECOURT	NOV			
	4th		Company at Rest.	
	5th	30 h	Company moved to BEAUFORT	
	6th	30 h	Coy Took over anti aircraft defence of AVENES Dump	
	7th		Coy Training	
			Coy moved to HAUTEVILLE	
	5th		Coy moved to LIENCOURT	

Johnson Lieut.
41st M.G.Coy

C O N F I D E N T I A L.

W A R   D I A R Y

- of -

41st B R I G A D E   M A C H I N E   G U N   C O M P A N Y.

From: 1st December, 1916.
To: 31st December, 1916.

Volume XI

WAR DIARY

INTELLIGENCE SUMMARY

Army Form C. 2118.

41st M.G. Coy

Place	Date	Hour	Summary of Events and Information	Remarks and references to Appendices
ENCOURT	1/12/16		Company training continues, and defence of AVESNES against hostile aircraft.	W.J.M.L. 2/Lieut.
"	13/12/16		Depôt of ammunition dump handed over to 105th M.G. Cy.	W.J.M.L.
"	14/12/16		Company marched to MONCHIET and billetted there.	W.J.M.L.
MONCHIET	15/12/16		Company marched to LE FERMONT and relieved the 37th M.G. Cy. in F Sector. Relief completed without casualties by 2 p.m.	W.J.M.L.
FERMONT	19/12/16		Inter-section relief carried out without event. 2/Lt. W.D. Trollope (15th Middlesex) joined company.	W.J.M.L. 2/Lt M.L.
"	23/12/16		Inter-section relief carried out. Nothing further to report.	W.J.M.L.
"	27/12/16		Captain J.E. Isaac (commanding) went on leave to U.K. Company commanded in his absence by Lieut. W.J.M.Litt	R./M.L.
"	29/12/16		Inter-section relief took place.	W.J.M.L.
"	30/12/16		Trenches in bad condition owing to continued rain.	W.J.M.L.
"	31/12/16		Nothing to report.	2/Lt M.L.

W.J.M.Litt Lieut.
for O.C. 41st M.G. Coy.

WAR DIARY
or
INTELLIGENCE SUMMARY. 41st Coy M.G.C.

Army Form C. 2118.

Place	Date	Hour	Summary of Events and Information	Remarks and references to Appendices
The Line.	28-3/1/18		Coy in the Line. Guns as follows :- 8 guns in Main resistance Trench for immediate defense purposes. Three guns are arranged to cross fire and have deep zones Barrage. Two guns in support line near junction of URVILLERS - ITANCOURT Road and ST QUENTIN - CHALONS Road. Two guns in front line and one in support are mounted for Anti-aircraft work by day, and have been frequently in action. Company H.Q. and Two support guns, which are close hedge as anything, were heavily shelled with 4.2 H.E shells on afternoon 30th inst.	a.b.f
	31/1/18		Transport camp moved from JUSSY to CLASTRES.	a.b.f.

A.B.Atcheson Capt.
o.c.

CONFIDENTIAL.

WAR DIARY

- of -

41st BRIGADE MACHINE GUN COMPANY.

From: 1st January, 1916.
To: 31st January, 1917.

Volume XI.

Army Form C. 2118.

4/th M.G.Coy

WAR DIARY
or
INTELLIGENCE SUMMARY.

(Erase heading not required.)

Instructions regarding War Diaries and Intelligence Summaries are contained in F. S. Regs., Part II. and the Staff Manual respectively. Title pages will be prepared in manuscript.

Place	Date	Hour	Summary of Events and Information	Remarks and references to Appendices
LE FERMONT	1/11/17		Resting & refit	
	4/11/17		Into section relief. 20 casualties	
	5/1/17		Emplacement obtained of 16 gun posts by 4.2" shell not near, no casualties	
			two	
	8/1/17		Into section relief	
	9/1/17		12000 rounds expended on indirect fire on enemy communication trenches & left front. Two guns were employed. There was no counter shift or s.o.s.	
			very short during day	
	10/11/17		O.C. Company returned from leave	
	12/11/17		Into section relief	
	13/11/17		New V5 emplacement completed	
	15/11/17		Into section relief. 1 O.R. wounded by shell fire at Coy H.Q.	
			snow during night	
	17/11/17		16 indirect fire emplacements begun in village lines	
	18/11/17		Rifle grenades went close to M.G. 3 gun during day	
	19/11/17		Into new emplacements completed	
	20/11/17		Into section relief	

H.V.M. Zich Lieut & Capt
Comdg 41st M.G. Coy

WAR DIARY
or
INTELLIGENCE SUMMARY.
(Erase heading not required.)

Army Form C. 2118.

41st M.G. Coy

Place	Date	Hour	Summary of Events and Information	Remarks and references to Appendices
ERMONT	24/1/17		Inter section relief. 4000 rounds fired indirect at FICHEUX during night	W.J.R.2.
	25/1/17		4000 rounds fired at FICHEUX	W.J.R.2.
	26/1/17		Enemy machine gun fire ceased at night	W.J.R.2.
	28/1/17		Inter section relief	W.J.R.2.
	29/1/17		Work held up by continued severe frost	W.J.R.2.
	31/1/17		Nothing to report	W.J.R.2.

W.J. McLean Lieut. to Capt.
comdg. 41st M.G. Coy

CONFIDENTIAL.

WAR DIARY

- of -

41st BRIGADE MACHINE GUN COMPANY.

From: 1st February, 1917.
To: 28th February, 1917.

Volume XII.

WAR DIARY
or
INTELLIGENCE SUMMARY.
(Erase heading not required.)

Army Form C. 2118.

Instructions regarding War Diaries and Intelligence Summaries are contained in F. S. Regs., Part II. and the Staff Manual respectively. Title pages will be prepared in manuscript.

Place	Date	Hour	Summary of Events and Information	Remarks and references to Appendices

WAR DIARY
or
INTELLIGENCE SUMMARY.

Army Form C. 2118.

Place	Date	Hour	Summary of Events and Information	Remarks and references to Appendices
ERNEVILLE	23/2/17 – 28/2/17			

CONFIDENTIAL.

WAR DIARY

- of -

41st MACHINE GUN COMPANY.

From: 1st March, 1917.
To: 31st March, 1917.

VOLUME XIII.

Army Form C. 2118.

WAR DIARY
or
INTELLIGENCE SUMMARY.
(Erase heading not required.)

41st. M.G. Coy.   Vol XIV

Place	Date	Hour	Summary of Events and Information	Remarks and references to Appendices
BERNEVILLE	1/3/17		No. 1 Section relieved No. 4 Section at the FOSSEUX air-guard, No. 2 Section relieved No. 3 Section at the GOUY air-guard, No. 3 Section took over working parties from No. 2 Section at GOUY. Headquarters and Transport moved to SOMBRIN where they were joined by No. 4 Section.	H.F.M.L.
SOMBRIN	2/3/17		2/Lieut A.D. Trollope and 2/Lieut M.H. Maggs reconnoitred the new relief by 42nd. M.G. Coy.	H.J.M.L.
"	3/3/17		Lieut. A.C.M. Dymock and 2/Lieut N.R. Itmis reconnoitred the new relief by 43rd. M.G. Coy.	H.J.M.L.
"	6/3/17		No. 4 Section relieved No. 2 Section at the GOUY air-guard No. 2 Section and No. 3 Section withdrew to SOMBRIN, the working party having discontinued	H.J.M.L.
"	13/3/17		No. 2 Section relieved No. 1 Section at the FOSSEUX air-guard, No. 3 Section relieved No. 4 Section at GOUY air-guard.	H.J.M.L.
"	14/3/17		Capt. D.E. Isaac and Lieut. H.J.M. Litoth reconnoitred the new relief by 42nd. and 43rd. M.G. Coys.	H.J.M.L.

WAR DIARY or INTELLIGENCE SUMMARY

Army Form C. 2118.

41st. M.G. Coy.

Place	Date	Hour	Summary of Events and Information	Remarks and references to Appendices
OMBRIN	15/3/17		Four riding horse returned to Mobile Veterinary Section under OB/1859 of 22/2/17	24/f.M.L.
"	16/3/17		Working party of 50 O.R. under 2/Lieut. M.R. Stones proceeded to FOSSEUX, also 1 Off and 20 O.R. of 41st. T.M. Battery and 30 O.R. of 8th K.R.R.C. under 2/Lieut Stones' command.	25/f.M.L.
"	17/3/17		One riding-horse contracted tetanus and was shot.	26/f.M.L.
"	20/3/17		Nos. 2 and 3 Sections relieved at FOSSEUX and GOUY ain-guards by 64th. M.G. Coy.	21/f.M.L.
"	22/3/17		Orders received to take over line held by 42nd and 43rd M.G. Coys. Company moved to BERNEVILLE. Working party at FOSSEUX also withdrawn to BERNEVILLE.	21/f.M.R.
BERNEVILLE	23/3/17		Gun limbers of nos. 1, 2, 3 Sections with one gun of no.4 Section proceeded by night to ARRAS.	21/f.M.L.
"	24/3/17		Company left BERNEVILLE at 9.30 a.m. and completed relief of the 42nd and 43rd. M.G. Coys. in the line S.E. of ARRAS by 2.0 p.m. Head-quarters and store teams of no.4 Section were billeted in ARRAS.	21/f.M.L. 21/f.M.R.

Army Form C. 2118.

WAR DIARY
or
INTELLIGENCE SUMMARY.

(Erase heading not required.)

41st. M.G. Coy.

Place	Date	Hour	Summary of Events and Information	Remarks and references to Appendices
ARRAS	28/3/17		3500 rounds fired during night to keep open gaps in wire made by artillery during the day	W.J.M.L
"	29/3/17		6000 rounds fired during night at gaps in enemy wire.	W.J.M.L
"	30/3/17		No 4 Section relieved No 3 Section in the line. One gun of no. 3 Section remained under O.C. No. 4. 18500 rounds fired during night on gaps in wire.	W.J.M.L

W.J. McIntosh Lieut. to Capt.
Comdg. 41st. M.G. Coy.

SECRET.

WAR DIARY

OF

41ST. MACHINE GUN COY.

From April 1st, 1917 to April 30th, 1917.

VOLUME 14.

Army Form C. 2118.

WAR DIARY
or
INTELLIGENCE SUMMARY.
(Erase heading not required.)

41 ST M.G. Coy

Instructions regarding War Diaries and Intelligence Summaries are contained in F. S. Regs., Part II. and the Staff Manual respectively. Title pages will be prepared in manuscript.

Place	Date	Hour	Summary of Events and Information	Remarks and references to Appendices
ARRAS	April 1st		Nos 1, 2 and 4 Sections in Trenches at H. Section ARRAS. No 3 in billets ARRAS	n.f.
	2nd		Guns employed in keeping open lanes in enemy's wire cut by artillery	n.f.
	3rd		Keeping lanes in wire open. Men under Para 30 left for FOSSEUX under LT DYMOCK. 3 P.M.	n.f.
	4th		Relieved during the day by 42nd + 43rd M.G. Coys. Relief completed the Company moved to the camp at RONVILLE. LT WJN LITTLE, LT JN DENNIS + 9 O.R. left ARRAS for new Transport Camp at BERNEVILLE	n.f.
RONVILLE	5th 6th 7th		Company in the camp RONVILLE in reserve to 42 + 43rd M.G. Coy.	n.f.
	8th		LT WJN LITTLE left BERNEVILLE for LESOUICH. Advanced Transport moved to ARRAS under LT NF PORTEOUS. In the camp RONVILLE	n.f.
	9th		Company moved to reserve position in Trenches 7.20 A.M. Pack animals at Battle Dump. 41st Brigade in support of 42nd + 43rd Brigades	n.f.
	10th	AT 11 A.M	Nos 1 + 4 Sections went forward under LT HEAL + 2nd LT BRETTELL to consolidate the COJEUL SWITCH. Nos 2 + 3 Section under 2nd LT MASS's + 2nd LT TROLLOPE moved to the HARP with guns on pack animals.	n.f.
		4 P.M.	Moved forward. No 3 Section relieved machine guns of 43rd + 13th at N 16 Central in BROWN LINE. 3 O.R. killed, 8 animals killed, 5 O.Rs wounded by shell fire. No 2 Section moved forward in support of Royal Battalion	n.f.

Army Form C. 2118.

WAR DIARY
or
INTELLIGENCE SUMMARY.
(Erase heading not required.)

41st Machine Gun Company

Place	Date	Hour	Summary of Events and Information	Remarks and references to Appendices
OJEUL SWITCH	April 10		2 guns under 2/Lt AMOS of N°1 Section ordered to the left battalion. N°4 Section ordered to the Right battalion. Captain ISAAC went forward with guns on the right.	n.f.
"	11th		N°1 Section had 3 O.R.s wounded. Captain ISAAC's morning. Command taken by Lt W.F. PORTEOUS. 3 P.M. 2 guns of N°1 Section withdrawn to Coy H.2. Guns on left front Lt. WANCOURT and at suspected M.G. emplacements. The Right Section gave covering support to infantry attacking WANCOURT + were also successful in keeping down enemy M.G. fire from positions in advance of village	n.f.
"	12th		10. A.M. The left Section moved guns forward to line N.17. A.1.8. to N.11.b.D.1.9. Covering advance projected between WANCOURT + GUEMAPPE. The 2 Section on the Right moved to positions on Northern + Southern slopes of Hill 90. + engaged enemy troops on opposite ridge in direction of WANCOURT Tower. Relieved at 5 A.M by 151st Machine Gun Company. Company moved to ARRAS.	n.f.
ARRAS	13th			n.f.
	14th		2.P.M. Company moved to BEAUMETS-LES-LOGES	n.f.
	15th		10.A.M. Company marched to SOMBRIN. Lt. LITTLE reported + took command of the Company.	n.f.

WAR DIARY
or
INTELLIGENCE SUMMARY.

(Erase heading not required.) 41st Machine Gun Company

Army Form C. 2118.

Place	Date	Hour	Summary of Events and Information	Remarks and references to Appendices
OMBRIN	April 16th to 22nd		Training in open warfare	M.T.
	23		" "	M.T.
	24		Company marched to BEINVILLERS.	M.T.
	25		8 A.M. Company marched to BLAIRVILLE	M.T.
	26		Company marched to MERCATEL. Rear party stayed at FICHEUX.	M.T.
	27		Company moved into Trenches. Transport moved to RENVILLE into LT STENBERG.	M.T.
	28		Rear party marched to MONCHIET.	M.T.
			2 Sections moved into front line trenches	M.T.

M Watsons W/m
O.C. 41st M.G.C.

MAP A — to accompany 14th Division Operation Order No. 112.

No 4

BEAURAINS

1. Creeping Barrage Lifts up to the Blue Line shewn thus — — — —

2. The figures 2.20 etc mean that the Creeping Barrage will lift from the line referred to at 2 hours 20 minutes after Zero, etc.

SCALE 1:10000

Confidential

41st M.G. Coy

War Diary for
May 1917

From: 1st May 1917
To: 31st May 1917

Volume XV

Vol 15

Shaw Capt
O/C 41st M.G. Coy

Army Form C. 2118.

WAR DIARY
or
INTELLIGENCE SUMMARY.
(Erase heading not required.)

Place	Date	Hour	Summary of Events and Information	Remarks and references to Appendices
	May			
ANCOURT	1st		Inter section relief post line trenches.	M.A. Capt. killed
do	2nd		Capt F.M. ARKLE assumes C.O. Joined details at MONCHIET	
do	3rd		The company assisted in the attack on the RED LINE, with 8PRs on the right and 9th K.R.R.C. on the left. When the 1st objective (BLUE LINE) had been captured 2nd Lieut AMOS took 49 men of No 1 and 2 men forward to the consolidation of when the 2nd objective (RED LINE) had been captured 2nd Lieut MAGGS was to move forward to their consolidation but not before ZERO + 43 hours. ZERO was 3-45 A.M. Lieut HEAL and 4 guns of No 4 sect to move into the front line (ISIS TRENCH) as a reserve. Lieut DYMOCK and 3 guns of No 2 section to move into support trench (EGRET TRENCH) as a support to come the ground in rear of front line. Owing to the division on both flanks being unable to take their objectives + bet flanks Q 14 D the being left in their render heavy M.G fire Nulla was force L.n.g.) near to the BROWN LINE. This was to right of front line. During this operation 3 OR. were killed, 8 OR wounded. 1 OR. missing + 2 OR wounded + missing. Lieut AMOS was recommended to the D.S.O. for great good during the action. The company moved to the support area N of MONCOURT when relieved by 13th M G Coy. The company moved to the 43rd Inf Bde.	M.A. killed
do	5th		The remained 3 days in support.	

Army Form C. 2118.

WAR DIARY
or
INTELLIGENCE SUMMARY.
(Erase heading not required.)

Instructions regarding War Diaries and Intelligence Summaries are contained in F. S. Regs., Part II. and the Staff Manual respectively. Title pages will be prepared in manuscript.

Place	Date	Hour	Summary of Events and Information	Remarks and references to Appendices
	May.			
HANCOURT	12th		Barometric Junction H.Q. by 43rd M.G. Coy. 2nd/Lt LITTLE	A.1
"	13th		Hostile officer reconnoitred our position in 185 Bn.t.	A.2
"	14th		Company commenced relief of 43rd M.G. Coy at 3.30 pm. Relief complete about 7.30 pm.	A.3
			LIEUT PORTEOUS remained in charge of men detailed for relief in support area.	
"	21st		One gun put out of action by enemy fire. Replaced same night. No cost gun put into trench.	A.4
"	24th		Company relieved by 42nd M.G. Coy. Relief complete by 8.30 pm. Company moves to support area for 48 hours during relief.	
FAVREUIL	25th		Company moved to Divisional Reserve camp at REAUMAISNIL. 1st took of arms the camp of 43rd M.G. Coy.	
"	29th		Owing to enemy airplanes flying at such a low altitude over our trenches 4 guns under LIEUT HEAL + 4 guns under 2nd/Lt TROLLOP moved up into concentrating in the trenches to confront enemy airplane attack.	A.5
"	31st		Line of 42nd M.G. Bde. East of HANCOURT. The 8 guns under LIEUT HEAL and 2/Lt TROLLOP returned in the evening.	A.6

J M Welsh Capt.
O.C. 41 M.G. Coy.

War Diary

41st. M.G. Coy.

June 1917

WAR DIARY or INTELLIGENCE SUMMARY

Army Form C. 2118.

41st. M.G. Coy.

Place	Date	Hour	Summary of Events and Information	Remarks and references to Appendices
BEAURAINS	1/6/17		Company in Divisional Reserve.	W.J. M.Z.
"	2/6/17		Lieut. M.E. Porteous, M.C. relieved the officer of the 43rd. M.G. Coy. in command of machine guns with the Divisional Artillery.	W.J. M.Z.
ANCOURT	4/6/17		Company went into Divisional Support, relieving 42nd. M.G. Coy. Relief completed by 8 p.m.	W.J. M.Z.
"	7/6/17		2/Lieut. W.R. Amos M.C. relieved Lieut. M.F. Porteous M.C. from B.1 (N29 b.1/5) B.2 (N28 b 95/90) B.3 (M 23 b 5/10) positions (Divl. artillery guard)	W.J. M.Z.
BEAURAINS	9/6/17		Company relieved about 8.0 p.m. by 169th. M.G. Coy. and withdrew to reserve camp, BEAURAINS, to which all guns withdrawn. B1, B2 being relieved by 4th. M.G. Coy. C position and B.3 by 169th M.G. Coy. Relief complete by 10 p.m.	W.J. M.Z.
"	10/6/17		Lieut. E.L. Bartleman and L.O.R. wounded by shell fire.	W.J. M.Z.
BEAUMETZ	11/6/17		Company moved at 5.45 a.m. to BEAUMETZ. C.S.M. Isaac accidentally shot.	W.J. M.Z.
AUDIEMPRÉ	12/6/17		Company moved at 8.30 a.m. to GAUDIEMPRÉ	W.J. M.Z.
LOUVENCOURT	13/6/17		Company moved at 5.20 a.m. to LOUVENCOURT	W.J. M.Z.
"	14/6/17		Company in training.	W.J. M.Z.
"	17/6/17		2/Lieut. E. Lamb and 2/Lieut. J. Mackie joined the company.	W.J. M.Z.
"	20/6/17		2/Lieut. E. Lamb left the company on cross-posting to 42nd M.G. Coy.	W.J. M.Z.

WAR DIARY
or
INTELLIGENCE SUMMARY.
(Erase heading not required.)

41st. M.G. Coy.

Army Form C. 2118.

Place	Date	Hour	Summary of Events and Information	Remarks and references to Appendices
LOUVENCOURT	27/6/17		Company took part in military Brigade Competitions.	11/J.32.
"	29/6/17		" " " " " "	11/J.32.
"	30/6/17		Company took part in Brigade Tactical Exercise at AUCHONVILLERS	11/J.32.

W.J.M.Litt Lieut. for Capt
comdg 41st M.G Coy.

Vol 17

War Diary

July 1917

41st. M.G.Coy

Volume XVII

WAR DIARY
or
INTELLIGENCE SUMMARY.
(Erase heading not required.)

41st M.G.C. Coy

Army Form C. 2118.

Place	Date	Hour	Summary of Events and Information	Remarks and references to Appendices
LOUVENCOURT	1/7/17		Company in training	7/7/17
BEAUVAL	10/7/17		Company moved to BEAUVAL. Capt. F.M. Arkle went on six leave to U.K. Company commanded in his absence by Lieut. L. Little.	7/7/17
DOULLENS	11/7/17		Company moved to DOULLENS and here entrained.	7/7/17
BERTHEN	12/7/17		Company detrained at GODESWAERVELDE and marched to billets near BERTHEN.	7/7/17
"	13/7/17		Company in training	7/7/17
"	15/7/17		Two guns under 2/Lieut. A.D. Trollope detailed for defence of E Siege Park Ammunition Dump at LOCRE.	7/7/17
"	17/7/17		Lieut. W.J.W. Little and 2/Lieut. W.R. Amos M.C. reconnoitred the WYTSCHAETE Ridge Defences.	7/7/17
"	18/7/17		Lieut. J.W. Heal and Lieut. F.L. Bartleman reconnoitred WYTSCHAETE Ridge Defences.	7/7/17
"	19/7/17		2/Lieut. A.D. Trollope relieved at LOCRE Dump by Lieut. F.L. Bartleman.	7/7/17
"	20/7/17		Lieut. J.N. Dennis and 2/Lieut. A.D. Trollope reconnoitred WYTSCHAETE Ridge Defences	7/7/17

Army Form C. 2118.

WAR DIARY
or
INTELLIGENCE SUMMARY. — 41st M.G. Coy.

(Erase heading not required.)

Place	Date	Hour	Summary of Events and Information	Remarks and references to Appendices
BERTHEN	23/7/17		Lieut. N.F. Porteous M.C. relieved Lieut. E.L. Barkman at LOCRE Dump. Lieut. N.J.N. Little reconnoitred front held by 41st Division. Capt. F.M. Arkle returned from leave.	
"	26/7/17		Company inspected by G.O.C. 2nd Army. Capt. F.M. Arkle and Lieut. N.J.N. Little reconnoitred part of front held by 19th Division. Lieut. W.F. Porteous M.C. relieved by 2/Lieut. J. Mackie.	
"	31/7/17		Orders received to proceed at an hour's notice to KEMMEL.	

W.J.N. Little
Lieut. for Capt.
Comdg. 41st. M.G. Coy

War Diary

41st. M.G. Coy.

August
1917

Volume XVIII

Army Form C. 2118.

WAR DIARY
or
INTELLIGENCE SUMMARY. 215th M.G. Coy.
(Erase heading not required.)

Place	Date	Hour	Summary of Events and Information	Remarks and references to Appendices
BERTHEN	1/8/17		Orders for move cancelled.	H.J.M.L.
"	2/8/17		Division becomes G.H.Q. Reserve	H.J.M.L.
"	6/8/17		Company marched to HONDEGHEM.	H.J.M.L.
HONDEGHEM	15/8/17		Transport left at 2 p.m. to proceed by road to DICKEBUSCH Area.	
			Company marched at 4.45 p.m. to CAESTRE, where they entrained for OUDER- DOM. On detraining Company marched to huts at 28 H 27 B 7/7. arriving 11.30 p.m.	
DICKEBUSCH	16/8/17		Transport rejoined Company. Company less two officers and 27 O.R. moved to CHATEAU SEGARD.	H.J.M.L.
HOOGE	15/8/17		Nos. 2 and 3 Sections moved into the line, relieving 169th M.G. Coy.	H.J.M.L.
"	19/8/17		Company in the line. No casualties.	H.J.M.L.
CHATEAU SEGARD	20/8/17		Sections in the line relieved by 43rd M.G. Coy. Company returned to Transport Rendezvous CHATEAU SEGARD.	H.J.M.L.
"	21/8/17		Nos. 1, 2, 4 Sections went up to line for barrage work, but could not get into action owing to successive heavy barrages.	H.J.M.L.
HOOGE	22/8/17		Nos. 1, 2, 4 Sections remained in their positions. 1 O.R. killed, 4 O.R. wounded	H.J.M.L.

Army Form C. 2118.

WAR DIARY
INTELLIGENCE SUMMARY
41st. M.G.Coy.

(Erase heading not required.)

Place	Date	Hour	Summary of Events and Information	Remarks and references to Appendices
HOOGE	23/8/17		Nos. 1 & 4 Sections withdrew to Transport Coop.	W.J.M.L.
DICKEBUSCH	24/8/17		Company moved to the Ecole on MENIN Road. Nos. 2 & 3 Sections relieved the 43rd. M.G.Coy in the line. 1 O.R. wounded.	W.J.M.L.
"	25/8/17		Company less 2 & 3 Sections withdrew to Transport Camp.	W.J.M.L.
"	26/8/17		Nos. 2 & 3 Sections relieved by 70th M.G.Coy, and withdrawn to Transport Camp. 5 O.R. killed, 7 O.R. wounded.	W.J.M.L.
"	27/8/17		Company moved to Ecole. 2/Lieut. A.D. Trollope wounded.	W.J.M.L.
"	28/8/17		Company withdrew to Transport Camp.	W.J.M.L.
"	29/8/17		Company proceeded by motor-lorry to billets in the METEREN Area. Transport moved by road.	W.J.M.L.
"	30/8/17		Company at rest near METEREN.	W.J.M.L.

W.J.M.Lith Lieut.
for Capt. comdg. 41st. M.G.Coy.

War Diary

September 1917

21st M.G. Coy

Volume XIX

WAR DIARY
INTELLIGENCE SUMMARY

Army Form C. 2118.

41st. M.G. Coy.

Place	Date	Hour	Summary of Events and Information	Remarks and references to Appendices
METEREN	1.9.17		Company in training near METEREN	W/D 2.
"	2.9.17		Company moved to HILLSIDE CAMP N. of NEUVE EGLISE and took over his from 42nd M.G. Coy	W/D 2.
NEUVE EGLISE	4.9.17		Capt. Arkle and Lieut. Little reconnoitred the machine gun posts of the 42nd M.G. Coy in the line.	W/D 2.
"	9.9.17		Company stood to in camp to reinforce in the event of an expected enemy raid.	W/D 2.
"	10.9.17		Company relieved 42nd M.G. Coy in the line. No.1 Section took the right sector, No.4 Section left sector. Relief was complete by 1 a.m. with 5 guns.	W/D 2.
MESSINES	11.9.17		Company in line. Enemy quiet apart from 20 casualties.	W/D 2.
"	13.9.17		2400 rounds fired on enemy roads and tracks during night.	W/D 2.
"	14.9.17		No.2 Section relieved No.1 Section, No.3 Section relieved No.4 Section. 2500 rounds fired on enemy tracks during night.	W/D 2.
"	15.9.17		2400 rounds fired on enemy tracks during night. Enemy aeroplane flew over low and MESSINES was driven off by the anti-aircraft gun at Coy. H.Q.	W/D 2.

WAR DIARY or INTELLIGENCE SUMMARY

41st M.G. Coy.

Army Form C. 2118.

Place	Date	Hour	Summary of Events and Information	Remarks and references to Appendices
MESSINES	16.9.17		No. 1 Gun was moved to a gun position on the right in the 8th Division area. 2500 rounds fired during night.	2/M 2
"	17.9.17		Nine barrage positions occupied during night. 8800 rounds were fired by five guns on roads and tracks. Nine guns were engaged in a barrage at 3 p.m. in conjunction with artillery. 18000 rounds were fired.	2/M 2
"	18.9.17		5750 rounds were fired during night. 18000 rounds were fired in conjunction with artillery barrage at 6 a.m. 2/Lieut. A.D. Trollope rejoined from hospital.	2/M 2
"	19.9.17		18 O.R. of no. 4 Section came up to Foley post in barrage at 20F.7500. rounds expended in harassing fire.	2/M 2
"	20.9.17		9250 rounds fired during night in harassing fire. 31,500 rounds were fired in barrage in conjunction with raid at 5.40 a.m. 1 O.R. wounded (copy). Coy was relieved by 43rd M.G. Coy - relief was complete by 11.30 p.m. Company returned to HILLSIDE CAMP.	2/M 2
NEUVE EGLISE	23.9.17		Company went into Divisional Reserve and became reserve for defence of ARMENTIERES	3/M 2
"	29.9.17		Lieut. J.W. Heal and 2/Lieut. A.D. Trollope were wounded (gas) and 1 O.R. killed and working party Capt. Arkle and Lieut. Little reconnoitred ARMENTIERES defences.	4/M 2

WAR DIARY or INTELLIGENCE SUMMARY

Army Form C. 2118.

41st. M.G.Coy.

Place	Date	Hour	Summary of Events and Information	Remarks and references to Appendices
EUVE EGLISE	25.9.17		Work begun on new Transport Lines for winter.	2/1/22
"	27.9.17		Working party of 2 off. and 50 O.R. worked at LA CRECHE Ammunition Dump.	2/1/22
"	28.9.17		2/Lieut. D.J. Gibson joined company. No. 4 Section relieved 4 Anti-aircraft guns at 42nd. M.G.Coy. and 2nd Section relieved three guns of 249th. M.G.Coy. and 1 gun of 43rd. M.G.Coy. in the line.	2/1/22
"	29.9.17		43rd M.G.Coy became responsible for defencement of ARMENTIERES Defences.	2/1/22

W.J.M.Litt. Lieut
for Capt. cond'g 41st. M.G.Coy.

CONFIDENTIAL.

41st M.G.Coy.

War Diary
October 1917

Volume XX

WAR DIARY
or
INTELLIGENCE SUMMARY
(Erase heading not required.)

Army Form C. 2118.

41st M.G. Coy.

Place	Date	Hour	Summary of Events and Information	Remarks and references to Appendices
Nieue Felse	1/10/17		Training & Sports in new Transport lines at Hillside Camp	
Dickenbusch	6/10/17		Coy marched to Rennighelst Lines	
			Remained until Coy moved to lines & on 9th	
			took over relieved	
	7/10/17		Lieut A.C.M. Spencer to Hospital sick	
	8/10/17			
Micmac Camp	9/10/17		Coy moved to Micmac Camp and remained	
	10/10/17		until Coy moved forward	
			Coy marched to Bedford House & relieved 15th & 13th Coy in front of	
Ridgewood	12/10/17		Gheluvelt Rd.	
	13/10/17		Coy in line	

WAR DIARY
INTELLIGENCE SUMMARY.   41st M.G. Coy

Army Form C. 2118.

(Erase heading not required.)

Place	Date	Hour	Summary of Events and Information	Remarks and references to Appendices
GHELUVELT	13.10.17		Coy in line. No casualties	WD
	14.10.17		Coy in line. No casualties. Lance Cpl [?] slightly wounded	
			Lieut T.H.G. Facey reported sick. Gas poison.	
	15.10.17		1 Driver killed, 3 wounded. 1 OR killed. 2 OR [?]	
			1 horse killed and 1 Pte Coy attached unit P3 Sec.	
	16.10.17		Ghan's Horse killed. Lieut [?] [?] to Coy HQ to [?] [?]	WD
	17.10.17		No 3 [?] [?] [?] [?] [?] [?] [?] [?]	WD
			[?] [?] [?] RIDGE WOOD [?] [?]	
			[?] [?] [?] [?] [?] [?] left of 10R	
			2 OR [?] [?] [?] [?] [?] [?]	
RIDGE WOOD			to 2 [?] [?] to 2 Coy returned to RIDGE WOOD	
			Riding entered by 9.30 a.m.	
	19.10.17		Coy moved to [?] [?] 1.35 p.m. [?] [?] [?]	
	20.10.17		43rd [?] attached	
DICKEBUSCH	22.10.17		Coy marched to CHIPPAWA CAMP arrived [?] [?]	
MEREN	23.10.17		Coy marched to MEREN [?] [?] [?]	

WAR DIARY or INTELLIGENCE SUMMARY

Army Form C. 2118.

41st M.G. Coy

Place	Date	Hour	Summary of Events and Information	Remarks and references to Appendices
METEREN	24/10/17		Capt F. M. Argles to Hospital sick. Lieut K.G. Whittaker assumed command	1.R.O.
"	25/10/17		2 Lt. G. Robbins reported from Base Depot	1.R.O.
"	26/10/17 to 31/10/17		Coy training. 11 O.R. from Base Depot reported 26.10.17	1.R.O.

K.G. Whittaker Lt
for Officer Commanding
41st M.G. Coy

Vol 21

War Diary

41st M.G. Coy

Nov. 30/17

Volume XXI

WAR DIARY
or
INTELLIGENCE SUMMARY

Army Form C. 2118.

210th Machine Gun Coy.

Place	Date	Hour	Summary of Events and Information	Remarks and references to Appendices
METEREN	1/10/17		Coy Training.	A.N.1 App.
"	2/10/17		Notification received that Capt. F.M. PARLE was transferred to base on 27/10/17.	A.B.1 App.
			LT. A.C.N. D'INGER arrived from Base.	
"	3/10/17		Coy Training in conjunction with 7th R.B. in BERTHEN Training area.	A.B.1 App.
			2/LT. L.G.P.H. RAYNER arrived from Base. LT. W.J.N. LITTLE appointed 2nd in command Coy.	
			Notification received of intended move of Division to TILQUES near ST OMER.	
"	4/11/17		Coy Training.	A.B.1 App
"	6/11/17		LT. W.J.N. LITTLE assumed vacant rank of Actg-Captain.	A/B.1 App.
"	8/11/17		Move to VAL D'ACQUIN as follows:- (1) Coy marched to CAESTRE STATION where entrained.	
"	11/11/17		Detrains at WIZERNES. March to VAL D'ACQUIN.	
			(2) Transport less Water-cart rolled out of G.S. Wagon by road night 11/12/11/17 at WALLON-CAPPEL, arrived VAL D'ACQUIN 12th.	A.B/App
			(3) Water-cart & rolled out G.S. Wagon by train to BAILLEUL WEST.	
			O/ZERNER from Base → Hosp. admitted to hospital.	
VAL D'- ACQUIN	12/11/17		{ Coy Training. 2/Lt. A.B. ACHESON arrived from Base → Hosp. admitted to hospital. 2/Lt. G. ROBBINS.	A.B./App
	13/11/17			

WAR DIARY

41st Machine Gun Coy.

Army Form C. 2118.

Instructions regarding War Diaries and Intelligence Summaries are contained in F. S. Regs., Part II. and the Staff Manual respectively. Title pages will be prepared in manuscript.

INTELLIGENCE SUMMARY.
(Erase heading not required.)

Place	Date	Hour	Summary of Events and Information	Remarks and references to Appendices
VAR D'REQUM	29/4/17		Orders received for move to BRANDHOEK and Wizernes to be proceed with. Transport and Advance-Guard + Watchment move forward to BRANDHOEK while the remainder on 30/4/17. Spent night 29-30 May at STEENVOORDE.	Appx 2
do.	30/4/17		Coy entrain at WIZERNES and proceed by train, detraining at BRANDHOEK & marched to camp at Goldfish Chateau.	Appx 2

Appendices Nos. 6

41st M. G. Coy

War Diary

December 1917

Volume XXII

WAR DIARY or INTELLIGENCE SUMMARY.

Army Form C. 2118.

41st Company Machine Gun Corps

Place	Date	Hour	Summary of Events and Information	Remarks and references to Appendices
GOLDFISH CHATEAU	1/10/17		Company at rest	A84
do.	2/10/17		Company less Transport move to "C" Camp WIELTJE. Transport remains at GOLDFISH CHATEAU.	A84
WIELTJE	3/10/17		Company relieved 212 M.G. Coy in the Line PASCHENDAELE Sector. 2 Guns in PASSCHENDAELE, 2 guns in MOSSELMARKT, 2 Guns in Pillbox at MEETCHEELE, 4 guns attached to 42 M.G. Coy for barrage purposes.	A84
WIELTJE and THE LINE	4/10/17		Coy in line. 1 O.R. wounded.	A84
	5/10/17		2 Guns moved from barrage positions to MEETCHEELE which is also extreme Coy H.Q. — These guns were again under command OP-C 41st Coy 112C.	A84
	6-7/10/17		Coy in line	A84
	8/10/17		From One gun under Major BARTLETT, moved to ABRAHAM HEIGHTS for purposes of 2nd line of defence according to orders of Corps M.G. Officer. Occupied bivouac on skyline amongst Field Artillery – no other cover was available. Arrived 11.0 a.m. – received direct hit on bivouac about half an hour later 2 O.R. killed 3 O.R. wounded.	A84
	9/10/17		Coy relieved early in morning and proceeded by Train and lorry to BRANDHOEK.	A84
BRANDHOEK	10-19/10/17		Coy in Rest at BRANDHOEK.	A84

Army Form C. 2118.

WAR DIARY
or
INTELLIGENCE SUMMARY.

(Erase heading not required.)

241st Company M.G.C.

Place	Date	Hour	Summary of Events and Information	Remarks and references to Appendices
BRANDHOEK	12/7/17		Lt E.I. BARTLEMAN to ENGLAND for interview (possible board of Indian Army.	AA9
do	13/7/17		Coy moved to 'C' Camp at WIELTJE. Transport to JUNCTION CAMP.	AA9
WIELTJE	14/7/17 15/7		Coy relieved 9 guns of 2nd/1st 4B M.G. Coy and 2 guns of 224 M.G. Coy in the Letter 2 guns attached to 42 M.G. Coy for barrage work. Remainder located as before except that two guns were located near NOREK FARM for defence in depth, and 3 guns only remained at Coy H.P.	AA9
LINE	15-17/7/17		Coy in line	AA9
do	18/7/17		2 guns at NOREK FARM relieved & withdrawn by 2/Lt J. MACRAE and 2 fresh teams. Guns at NOREK FARM moved forward to positions near ERWIN HOUSE.	AA9
do	2/8/17		Details camp moved from WIELTJE to JUNCTION CAMP and takes our camp-from No 224. Company in a very bad condition. 1 O.R. gassed.	AA9
Posted 25/11/17 – 31/8/17			Under orders from Corps much harassing fire was carried out during the period as under 6.0 am 10/15 – 6.0 am 18/8, 100 rnds each Target VOLT FARM, VENISON TRENCH, MALLET COPSE 6.0 am 19/8 – 6.0 am 20/8, 75 rnds each do do WRATH FARM, also 150 rnds each SOUTHERN FARM.	CAA9

Army Form C. 2118.

WAR DIARY
or
INTELLIGENCE SUMMARY.
(Erase heading not required.)

MIOTTE M&E

Instructions regarding War Diaries and Intelligence Summaries are contained in F. S. Regs., Part II. and the Staff Manual respectively. Title pages will be prepared in manuscript.

Place	Date	Hour	Summary of Events and Information	Remarks and references to Appendices
JUNCTION CAMP	22-27/4/17		During the night Coy relieved by 413 M.G. Coy. Proceeded to JUNCTION CAMP under Dublin Bdes. 3 gun teams kept in perpetual readiness to move at a moments notice under O.C. 163 PORTEOUS M.C. & further Orders or on Lantoshe Switch (BRANDNSTAPEL — SWITCH).	A84 A84
do.	23/4/17		Coy at rest. 3 emergency guns based on STRAZELE Coy.	A84
do.	24/4/17		Transport and stores moved on two days journey via ZERMEZEELE to VAL D'ACQUIN. Longvink & hutting built, & tents also moved direct to VAL D'ACQUIN.	A84
do.	25/4/17		Company entrained at ST JEAN and proceeded to WIZERNES, thence by lorry to VAL D'ACQUIN.	A84
VAL D'ACQUIN	26-31/4/17		Training with Lewis Company Arms Drill 31/4/17.	A84

ABSpencer Capt.
O. C.

Vol 23

41st Machine Gun Coy.

War Diary

January 1918

Volume XXIII

Army Form C. 2118.

WAR DIARY
or
INTELLIGENCE SUMMARY. — 41st Coy Machine Gun Corps.

(Erase heading not required.)

Instructions regarding War Diaries and Intelligence Summaries are contained in F.S. Regs. Part II. and the Staff Manual respectively. Title pages will be prepared in manuscript.

Place	Date	Hour	Summary of Events and Information	Remarks and references to Appendices
VAL D'ACQ	1/1/18		Coy Training in billets.	AQAF
do	2/1/18		Move to TATINGHEM under Brigade orders preparatory to entrainment at ST. OMER.	AQAF
TATINGHEM	3/1/18		Entrained at ST OMER STATION for FREE MILL after its embassy arrival detrained and marched to	AQAF
SAULTY-LE-SEC	4/1/18		SAULTY - LE - SEC. Transferred from Fourth Army to Fifth Army.	AQAF
do	5/1/18		Training for Trench Warfare begins. Courses in Field Engineering, Gas, wiring, Physical Training etc arranged.	AQAF
do	6/1/18		2/Lt. J. MACKIE to Camiers for a course.	AQAF
do	4-21 Jan/18		In Training	AQAF
do	22/1/18		Company and Transport marched to FRESNOY - EN - CHAUSSEE	AQAF
FRESNOY-EN-CHAUSSEE	23/1/18		Company and Transport marched to ROYE where billeted for the night.	AQAF
ROYE	24/1/18		Company and Transport marched to BEINES and billeted for the night.	AQAF
BEINES	25/1/18		Company and Transport marched to JUSSY and billeted. CAPT. A.B. ACHESON proceeds to Reconnoitre the Line preparatory to taking over from the French.	AQAF
JUSSY	26/1/18		Ammunition sent up to Gun position in the Line. - Wt action of Divisional Front - immediately in	LBAF
			Avance DURVILLERS. Coy proceeded to Dugouts at Station ESSIGNY - LE - GRAND.	
JUSSY	27/1/18		Company relieves 411th th Regt of French Army in the Line. Relief successfully accomplished during very quiet night. Relief carried out	MBAF

War Diary
February 1918

41st M.G. Coy

Volume XXIV

WAR DIARY
or
INTELLIGENCE SUMMARY

Army Form C. 2118.

41. ey. Machine Gun Corp.

Place	Date	Hour	Summary of Events and Information	Remarks and references to Appendices
LINE	1/2/18		Coy in the lines. Everything quiet in Divisional Front.	LRA
"	2/2/18		E.A. engaged frequently by our A.A. guns	LRA
"	5/2/18		Lieut. W.J.R. Little leave to U.K. Capt. R.B. Aitchison in comd.	
			No 1 Section relieved No 4 Section. 2 guns No 2 Section, 2 guns No 3 Section in line	LRA
"	6/2/18		E.A. engaged frequently by our A.A. guns. 2 Lt Mackie returns from Camiers & R.A.	LRA
"	9/2/18		E.A. engaged frequently by our A.A. guns. Up to this, there existed in the only front line by an avns coming into the Lens Region	
			for protection to strafe refugees	LRA
"	11/2/18		No 4 Section relieves No 3 Section. 2 guns No 2 & 2 and of No 4 Section	LRA
"	12/2/18		One night gun in PICHING heavy punched by right & tail cover parties on BATTLE ZONE	LRA
			6 guns in reserve allotted definite positions in BATTLE ZONE	
"	17/2/18		No 3 Section relieved No Section. 2 guns Lough-Inch-Co. URUMBER? refuse.	LRA
			2 guns of No 2 Section relieves 2 guns of No 4 Section. 2 Lt RAYNER to UK	LRA
"	21/2/18		Lieut. W.J.R. Little from leave & assumes command.	LRA
"	23/2/18		No 1 Section relieves No 4 Section. 2 guns No 2 Section relieves 2 guns of No 2 Section	LRA
"	24/2/18		5700 rounds expended fired on aeroplanes near TANCOURT.	LRA

Army Form C. 2118.

WAR DIARY
or
INTELLIGENCE SUMMARY.
(Erase heading not required.)

41st Coy Machine Gun Corps.

Place	Date	Hour	Summary of Events and Information	Remarks and references to Appendices
	24/4/18		Capt A.B. ACHESON appointed Adjutant. Lieut STEENBERG appointed T.O. of the 14th Divnl M.G. Battalion.	WRA
	25/4/18		5000 rounds harassing fire on target: OLD MILL north of MANCOURT. Own infantry complained of our fire being too short but were able to satisfy the officers sent to investigate — that supply elevens were being harrassed. Withdrew 2 guns from our Coy HQ to strong point near Coy Battalion HQ	WRA
	26/4/18		2 O.R. reported as reinforcements from M.G. Base Depot.	WRA
	27/4/18		Withdrew left gun in MAER to position in FRANCE ALLEY. Working on dug outs in RUSSIAN TRENCH so that accommodation can be provided for two teams. Gun position of these teams to be in OBSERVERS WORK	WRA
	28/4/18		Lieut A.M. DYMOCK to U.K. for monthly special leave. Enemy shelled back areas with precautionary action term in BATTLE ZONE.	WRA

W R Amos 2/Lt.
for Capt. Commanding
41st M.G. Coy

www.ingramcontent.com/pod-product-compliance
Lightning Source LLC
Chambersburg PA
CBHW081444160426
43193CB00013B/2380